Digital Photography

For the Crime Scene Investigator

By Jon Freivald, CCSA

Mountain Cabin Multimedia

ISBN: 978-0692429112

Published by:

Mountain Cabin Multimedia
400 Cabell Mountain Lane
Arrington, Va 22922

Mountain Cabin Multimedia   Printed in the United States of America

A note to the reader:

Experienced general practitioner, professional, or other non-crime scene photographers may very well look at this book and state that I oversimplify some concepts and techniques. I counter that over four decades of photographic experience have been distilled to: "cut-to-the-chase, what do I need to know to get the job done?" Yes, there is a huge amount of theory and many more techniques available to a photographer, but as they apply to crime scene photography, they simply muddy the waters. There are many excellent books and web sites dedicated to the artistic side of photography. That is not the purpose of this book. This book is intended to give you, the crime scene investigator *who is not a professional photographer*, the fundamentals and bulletproof techniques you need to do the job.

Crime Scene Investigators,

Solving Crime Through Science

Dedicated to the victims.

Contents

Preface

Modern digital cameras are amazing. They range from computers with cameras, like an iPhone, to incredibly expensive professional grade instruments that happen to be computerized, like a Nikon D4S, a Canon EOS-1D C or a Hasselblad H5D-50c, and an entire gamut in between. They come in many sizes, capabilities and formats. They also range in price from a $20 Vivitar point-and-shoot to over $36,000 for the above-mentioned Hasselblad!

What they all have in common is that just about anyone can pick one up, turn it on, and take a pretty good snapshot. These cameras are smart. They meter, they measure, they compare and they focus all in an instant, and the results are such that the everyday shutterbug is nearly always happy with the results. Crime scene photography, however, is not simply taking snapshots. We need capabilities above the average point-and-shoot camera. We even need capabilities above some of the consumer grade entry-level DSLR cameras. We need cameras that let us take manual control of most aspects of the photography process.

So why *another* photography book? It started as a conversation with a fellow Evidence Technician when they asked me about a particular photography problem they were experiencing. I showed them something that I had *assumed* (yes, I know) that everybody knew and watched a light bulb come on. Another Tech joined the conversation and it quickly became clear that most of us were setting "A" for auto and rolling the dice. The fact that we had been getting the good results we had was a testament to the state of technology with digital cameras plus a huge dose of collective luck! I started outlining basic fundamentals to put together a "cheat sheet" for our team and was quickly presented with follow-on questions. I started to put together a lesson plan but decided that what we really needed was a quick-reference that we could carry with us in our kits. I looked at my library. I looked online. I consulted with others. I found three basic categories of materials available: general photography books that did not address the issues we encounter working crime scenes; crime scene books that were generally pretty expensive, some of which barely touched on photography; and material that was outdated, irrelevant (like types of film!) material, or just plain wrong material. Yes, there are a number of very good crime scene photography books – I own several, and have read more. What I was not looking for, however, was something I might be able to convince the department to purchase one of, or something that was 90% background and theory and only 10% how-to. I was looking for something that would be succinct, cover the areas we need, and both small and inexpensive enough that we could put one in every kit for every Tech. I also wanted it to be simple enough that a neophyte could pick it up, put together a kit, and start taking some basic pictures pretty much immediately. I started fleshing out the lesson plan. I focused on the what and the how, leaving the why, the theory and the history out of the way. As projects usually do, this one took on a life of its own and grew to the point that I decided I needed to put it together in book form. If I was going to go that far, I would make it available to our brothers and sisters in blue as inexpensively as possible.

By the time you finish reading this book, you will know what capabilities you need, and be able to select a camera and ancillary equipment to suit your needs. I will not make brand or model recommendations, nor will I recommend a vendor, as that would have the effect of starting a religious war, to no avail (does SureFire vs. Streamlight ring a bell?). There are a lot of brands and a lot of cameras out there that will function perfectly well.

Law enforcement personnel, as we all know, are not made of money. Neither are most of our agencies. We don't need a Hasselblad to do excellent crime scene work. Starting from scratch in today's market, staying with all new equipment, a frugal buyer can put together a perfectly adequate kit tailored for high quality crime scene photography for around $1,000. Shopping used or reconditioned gear can save even more.

As with any skill, practice and experience will improve your craft. Take the time to work through these concepts with your own equipment so you get to the field ready to take excellent photographs.

I hope you find this book useful and use what you learn here to bring many criminals to justice. Feedback, questions & comments are all welcome.

Jon Freivald
Arrington, Virginia
February 2015
jon@freivald.org

Digital Photography

For the Crime Scene Investigator

Photography is writing (graphy) with light (photo). Digital is pertaining to, or using data in the form of numerical digits. Digital photography is using tools (digital camera, lenses, etc.) to capture light onto a digital medium (sensor) to create a data file containing an image.

Crime Scene Photography is the application of basic photographic principles in a systematic manner in order to create a complete, high quality visual record of the entire crime scene, all evidence, and other key aspects of the investigation.

Who should read this book?

Evidence Technicians, Forensic Technicians, Detectives, Investigators; whatever the title you wear, if you use photography to document crime scenes and evidence, this book is for you. While written specifically to *The Systematic Approach*, as taught by the *Virginia Department of Forensic Science* and many other places, the fundamentals and concepts covered in this book apply equally well in any methodology.

What is this book about?

Any good investigator is going to document a crime scene with notes, sketches and photographs. The purpose of the photographs are: to provide a permanent visual record of the scene and evidence; to assist in the preparation of reports; to refresh memory; to substantiate testimony; to clarify understanding; and to allow for outside analysis. To be admissible in court, photographs must be accurate, authentic and relevant.

This book will take the reader through photography fundamentals, apply them to crime scene work, and tie everything together. Very little theory is covered. To get the job done you need the how, not the why. It is also intended to be a reference you can carry with you in the field. The files referenced in this book can be found online at http://tinyurl.com/maube4r and loaded to your computer, tablet or smartphone[1].

It will cover the equipment needed, as well as equipment that is nice to have, how to use it, and how to obtain accurate, relevant and useful photographs of crime scenes and evidence. It will also identify common problems typically encountered and how to overcome them. By the time you the reader have mastered the techniques covered in this book, you will be able to take the best crime scene and evidence photographs that any investigator, prosecutor or juror could ask for.

---

[1] The spreadsheets require Microsoft Excel to function properly. As of this writing, Excel is available free of charge for tablets and smartphones.

Digital Photography for the Crime Scene Investigator

Some Cardinal Rules before we start.

These are important enough to cover here in the very beginning.

1. NEVER, never, ever, ever, ever, (no, this is *not* a Taylor Swift song!) delete a photo while you are shooting a crime scene. It doesn't matter how bad it is – blurry, dark, washed out, whatever – a bad photo is a bad photo, but a missing photo is an opportunity for a defense attorney to attack the "missing exculpatory evidence that was in that photo." Do not let this happen to you.
2. Your end goal is to get good photographs right off the camera. Sometimes, however, you may need to edit an image[2] to correct exposure or contrast. When a photograph needs editing, the *very first step* is making a copy of the original and doing your work *only* on the copy. You should NEVER be selecting "File/Save" while you have an original file open. Always start your editing session with "File/Save As" and changing the filename.

---

[2] There are so many editing tools available that it is well beyond the scope of this book to detail any specific editing processes.

Equipment

Your agency (or your wallet) will determine if you have a photography kit assigned to you or if there is one that is shared by several people or even everybody in the agency. No matter the situation, the following list is a minimum kit:

DSLR[3] Camera	Flash	6" grey scale
Battery	Flash Batteries	"Bureau" scale
Battery charger	Remote flash cord	ABFO #2 scale
Memory card	Modeling clay or Play-doh	Camera bag
Lens[4]	Tripod	
Cable release (locking)	Line or hot-shoe level	

Additional items to round out a well outfitted kit include:

Spare camera battery(ies)	6" white scale	Screw-on Orange filter
Spare memory card(s)	6" black scale	Screw-on Yellow filter
Memory card reader	6" clear scale	Screw-on Red filter
Screw-on UV filter[5]	6" orange/fluorescent scale	Gaffer's tape
Lens cleaning cloth	Disposable scale cards	Masking tape
Air brush (simple bulb type)	Scale tape	White (medical type) tape
Close-up rings or Macro lens	Small (12-25') tape measure	Self-adhesive labels
"Fun-tack" or similar putty	Cardboard "tent" markers	Portrait lens[6]
Plastic pointers	High output LED light	

Some items that are used infrequently enough that many agencies only maintain one of each and everyone shares them. Typically these items are stored at a central location.

Prime (fixed) lens	Work lights	Trajectory lasers
Blood sticks	Snow wax	Laser fog
Light table	Light shed	Panoramic head

The list could go on and on, but these items will get the job done, and done well.

---

[3] DSLR is an acronym for Digital Single Lens Reflex. The SLR portion means you are actually looking through the lens when you are composing your image, focusing, etc. Point-and-shoot cameras do not have the level of control available that we need for this type of photography.
[4] For a "DX" or APS format camera this should be an 18-55mm zoom lens. For an "FX" or full frame format camera, this should be a 24-85mm zoom lens.
[5] At about $10, this is the cheapest lens insurance you can buy. Put it on. Leave it on.
[6] 85mm for DX or 120 to 135mm for FX.

Concepts

Initially, we need to cover some basic photography concepts. Once we have done that, we will put them together and relate them to crime scene work and the systematic approach.

Focal Length

Techno-speak: The focal length of a lens is the distance from the optical center of the lens to the sensor when the lens is focused on infinity.

What it means to you: Focal length affects the *apparent* magnification of a lens, and the angle/field of view. It is expressed in millimeters, such as a 35mm lens.

Lenses that come closest to a 45° angle field of view "see what the eye sees" and are considered the *normal* lens for that camera. For "DX" format cameras, this is a 35mm lens. For "FX" format cameras, this is a 50mm lens.

A shorter (smaller) focal length will have a wider field of view and "less magnification" while a longer (larger) focal length will have a narrower field of view and "more magnification".

Prime lenses have a single focal length. Zoom lenses cover a range of focal lengths. For most crime scene work, a standard "kit lens" zoom adequately covers the range we need. On a DX format camera the typical lens is 18-55mm. This gives an 18mm wide-angle setting, a 35mm Normal Lens setting, and a 55mm full zoom setting. An FX format kit lens is typically 24-85mm, giving us a 24mm wide-angle, a 50mm Normal Lens, and an 85mm full zoom setting. Either lens will also adjust to any other setting in their range.

Exposure

Exposure is the result of the amount of light entering the camera and its affect on the sensor. The volume of light is controlled by the size of the aperture. The time light is allowed into the camera is controlled by the shutter speed. The ISO sensitivity setting controls the intensity of the sensors reaction to light. Finally, light can be augmented by flash and other means.

"Correct" exposure is the combination of settings that captures detail in all areas of the photograph, from the darkest shadows to the brightest highlights. In some circumstances, multiple images are necessary to properly expose an area or item.

Stops

A "stop" in photography is the halving or doubling of light. Aperture size, shutter speed and ISO sensitivity are all designated in stop or partial stop values. This is explored in more detail in the section on Reciprocal Exposure starting on page 7.

Aperture

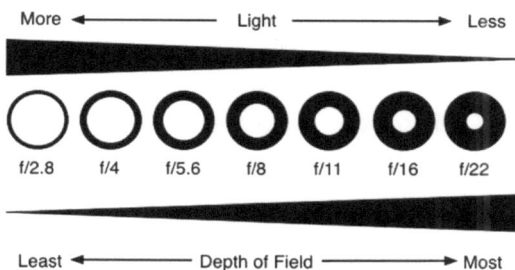

The aperture is the opening in the lens through which light passes. It is controlled by a circular diaphragm and is designated with a numeric value. Each numeric value shown in the diagram above is one stop. These values are called the "f/stop" and are designated with the notation of a small f followed by a slash followed by the numeric value, such as f/8. The whole stop values in the diagram are called "primary" f/stops. The aperture is typically set by a ring at the base of the lens or a command dial.

Shutter

The shutter is a light blocking barrier that opens for a specific period of time. Each time you halve or double the speed, you halve or double the amount of light, which is one stop of adjustment. The time value the shutter is set to is expressed in seconds or fractions of a second. Speeds that are fractions of a second are displayed as whole numbers. For example, $1/60^{th}$ of a second will display as 60 and $1/125^{th}$ of a second will display as 125. Speeds that are a full second or longer are displayed as a decimal number with a tic-mark notation. For example, 5 seconds will display as 5" and 2 ½ seconds will display as 2.5".

Once you exceed the time capability of your camera (typically 30 seconds) there is a special mode called "Bulb". In this mode you the photographer holds the shutter open for an arbitrary amount of time. The time the shutter is open is now controlled by you, not the camera. To eliminate camera shake, a locking cable release must be used. Some Nikon cameras have an additional setting labeled "Time". In this mode the first activation of the shutter release opens the shutter. The shutter will remain open until the shutter is released again, or 30 minutes, whichever is first. This mode allows the use of a non-locking release such as the ML-L3 infrared remote, or even, with great care, pressing the actual shutter button on the camera itself.

When your shutter speed is below 1/60th of a second, you need to use a tripod to eliminate camera shake causing your image to blur. When you are using flash, it needs to be at or slower than your camera's sync speed[7]. If there is movement in your frame, you will need a faster shutter speed to freeze it (see the shutter speed table in the Rules of Thumb section).

Shutter speed is nearly always set using a command dial.

ISO sensitivity

The ISO sensitivity setting determines how sensitive to light the sensor is. The values are expressed numerically and each time the value is halved or doubled, the amount of light in the image is halved or doubled (are you sensing a pattern here?). Typically used values are 100 and 400, though cameras today go to 12,800 or even higher. The lower the ISO setting, the finer the detail in the resulting image. Increasing the ISO increases the sensor's sensitivity to light, but at the cost of it's being able to record fine detail. The higher the ISO, the more detail is lost. The older the technology used in the camera, the more pronounced this effect will be. The ISO sensitivity is typically set via a menu, a dedicated button, or a button and command dial combination.

Metering

Your camera displays an exposure meter in any of the manual or semi-manual modes. You are properly exposed (did you tuck in your shirt?) when the meter is at the center point, as in the center photo in the figure at the top of the facing page. There are generally three metering modes. These are Matrix, Center Weighted, and Spot.

- Matrix metering selects what it assumes is the best exposure for the scene by dividing the frame into a matrix of select pixels, metering each matrix pixel, and comparing the values to an internal scene database.
- Center weighted metering measures the exposure for the entire frame (as one entity) and then measures the exposure for the center area of the frame. It then calculates a weighted average with emphasis given to the center of the frame.
- Spot metering measures the exposure value in a small circle centered on the selected focus point. It is normally used when you have a large variation in the frame, so you spot meter the critical areas and use the combined values to determine your final exposure setting.

---

[7] Most cameras will automatically select 1/60th of a second as the shutter speed when a flash unit is detected.

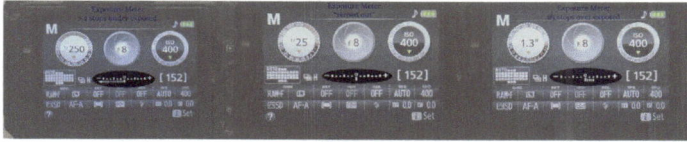

This illustration shows the exposure meter indicating under exposure (left), proper exposure (center) and overexposure (right).

When the camera is metering, it is assuming that your scene will average the reflectivity of "middle grey[8]" and reflect 18% of the available light. For many scenes, this assumption is appropriate. For others, however, it is not, so the scene fools the camera's meter. Examples would include a black coat on a black couch or highly reflective surfaces such as snow filling the majority of the frame. In a counter-intuitive manner, you need to *decrease* your exposure for dark subjects and *increase* your exposure for light subjects. How much depends on how dark or light the subject is. In general, start with one full stop and adjust from there after examining the results.

Reciprocal Exposure

All of the factors that affect exposure are reciprocal. Each element is measured in *stops* of light. A *stop* of light is the halving or doubling of light. Doubling your light increases your exposure 1 stop. Cutting your light in half decreases your exposure 1 stop. If you have a properly exposed image but need to decrease your aperture 2 stops to get adequate *depth of field* (explained in detail later), you can increase any one of the other factors (shutter speed, ISO sensitivity, or flash output) 2 stops to return to the same overall exposure. Increasing 2 factors 1 stop each gives, yet again, the same result.

The terms increase and decrease are not intuitive when you are making exposure adjustments. You first need to know what each adjustment does, and then apply the term "increase" in context to mean "add more light," while decrease means "take light away." Reduce the shutter speed to increase exposure. Reduce the aperture setting, which enlarges the hole, to increase exposure. This is not intuitive because our minds automatically think that a bigger number means more, yet in both of these cases, the bigger the number, the less the light. Yes, f/8 is a much bigger hole than f/22, and 1/125th second is faster than 1/60th second, reducing the light, though our brain's normal convention would tell us otherwise. *To eliminate confusion, always say you are increasing or decreasing the exposure in relation to what you are doing to the light, not the specific control you are adjusting. Decreasing stops decreases exposure, making the image darker, and increasing stops increases exposure, making the image brighter.*

---

[8] Middle grey is the tone on a grey scale that is half-way between full black and full white.

As an example, you meter a scene and come up with ISO 400, f/8 aperture and 1/250th second shutter speed as the correct exposure. You then calculate your *depth of field* (you will see how later) and determine you need an f/16 aperture. The difference between f/8 and f/16 is 2 stops (you can refer to the chart on page 35). If you simply change your f/stop to f/16, you will be 2 stops under exposed (dark). Increasing your f/stop decreased your exposure. Now, to get back to a correct exposure, you need to increase your exposure the same 2 stops. You could increase your ISO 2 stops to 1600;. You could decrease your shutter speed 2 stops to 1/60th second; or you could increase your ISO 1 stop to 800 and reduce your shutter speed 1 stop to 1/125th second. All of these are functionally equivalent:

1. ISO 400, f/8, 250
   a. Our "baseline" or starting point.
2. ISO 1600, f/16, 250
   a. 400 to 1600 = +2 stops, f/8 to f/16 = -2 stops for a net zero.
3. ISO 400, f/16, 60
   a. f/8 to f/16 = -2 stops, 250 to 60 = +2 stops for a net zero.
4. ISO 800, f/16, 125
   a. 400 to 800 = +1 stop, f/8 to f/16 = -2 stops, 250 to 125 = +1 stop for a net zero.

As you will see, we would find option #3 the most desirable for what we do, but the actual exposure would be the same for all 4.

Bracketing

Bracketing is a methodology where you determine an exposure and then take additional photos with the exposure adjusted in both directions. You might do this because you were unsure of getting the correct exposure. Another reason to do this would be an image where proper exposure of the middle tones would leave the highlights washed out, and the shadows murky black blobs with no detail. By bracketing you would have 3 (or more) images showing the mid-tones, the highlights, and the shadows, all in acceptable detail. The size of the bracket is determined by the photographer both in the amount of adjustment between the shots, and the number of shots taken on either side of the original exposure. Bracketing requires the camera to be in manual mode, which is explained later.

For example, to bracket one stop by a full stop in each direction from f/8 at 250, you would take the following photos:

1. f/8 at 250 (the original exposure)
2. f/8 at 125 or f/5.6 at 250 (+1 stop)
3. f/8 at 500 or f/11 at 250 (-1 stop)

Alternately, to bracket one stop in 1/3 stop increments, you would take the following photos:

1. f/8 at 250 (the original exposure)

2. f/8 at 200 or f/7.1 at 250 (+1/3 stop)
3. f/8 at 160 or f/6.3 at 250 (+2/3 stop)
4. f/8 at 125 or f/5.6 at 250 (+1 stop)
5. f/8 at 320 or f/9 at 250 (-1/3 stop)
6. f/8 at 400 or f/10 at 250 (-2/3 stop)
7. f/8 at 500 or f/11 at 250 (-1 stop)

Other than the exposure settings, the photos in each sequence are identical. Focus, framing, composition, focal length – everything remains the same from shot to shot during the bracket. In general, for crime scene work, you will bracket using the shutter speed so the f/stop and depth of field remain constant.

As you can see, doing this and keeping track of it manually can be tedious, especially if you have a lot of shots you need to bracket. Many cameras have an automatic bracketing mode. Consult your manual to determine if your camera has this feature and how to access it.

Focus

Focus is defined as the point at which light rays converge to give a clear and sharply defined image of a given subject. The size of the circle of light that appears to the eye to be a focused point is called the *circles of confusion*.

There are two possible types of focusing you will be concerned with; which one is determined by the type of photo you are taking in any given situation.
- For Overall & Midrange photographs, you will be concerned with the overall area of the image that is in focus. For this you will learn to calculate Depth of Field and Hyperfocal Distance.
- For close-up photographs you will be concerned with the focus being absolutely crisp on the item or detail you are photographing, much less concerned with Depth of Field, and unconcerned with Hyperfocal Distance.

Lack of focus can make an image appear unprofessional or even render it useless.

There are several auto-focus settings, ranging from dynamic focus based on multiple sampled areas in the frame to single point focus. In our case, the single point mode should be chosen. With any other setting, you do not control the focal point, which means you do not control Depth of Field.

When the focus point is not in the middle of the frame, you can still use auto-focus two ways:
1. Select the focal point that corresponds to the correct location in the frame. With most cameras you do this with the multi selector on the back of the camera.
2. Place the active focal point on the point of focus, depress the shutter half way and let focus lock. Then, without releasing the shutter, re-frame the image and finish pressing the shutter.

To manually focus, there may be a switch on the camera body or lens, or you may have to make a menu selection. Once in manual focus mode, use the focus ring on the lens. In this mode, the focus indicator in the viewfinder will still work in most cameras.

Before using manual focus, or if auto-focus does not look crisp to you through the viewfinder, adjust the diopter for your eyes. Set the camera up on a tripod so it is perpendicular to a flat but complex subject[9] and allow auto-focus to lock on it. Then, looking through the viewfinder, adjust the diopter knob (shown here, located just to the right of the viewfinder on a Nikon D5300) until the image appears to be in sharp focus. If you can't quite get sharp focus, learn to use the focus indicator in the viewfinder. You should only have to adjust the diopter once per camera unless you share with someone who's vision is different than yours.

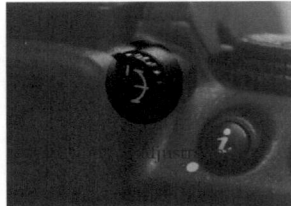

Depth of Field

Depth of Field is the distance from the closest object in a photograph to the farthest object which are both in acceptable focus.

When photographing a crime scene, a general rule is that the photographer must always strive to obtain the greatest depth of field possible in every photograph.

Three factors affect Depth of Field. They are:
1. Aperture – Smaller apertures (smaller opening, larger f/stop designation) produce more depth of field than larger apertures (larger opening, smaller f/stop designation).
2. Focal Length – The shorter (smaller) the focal length, the greater the depth of field.
3. Focus Distance – The farther away the point of focus, the greater the depth of field.

---

[9] Such as a page of text, a scale card, a checkerboard pattern, etc.

The following diagram shows the effect of Depth of Field on an image. The shading indicates the Depth of Field, or area in acceptable focus, for each f/stop. (For illustration only, not to scale.)

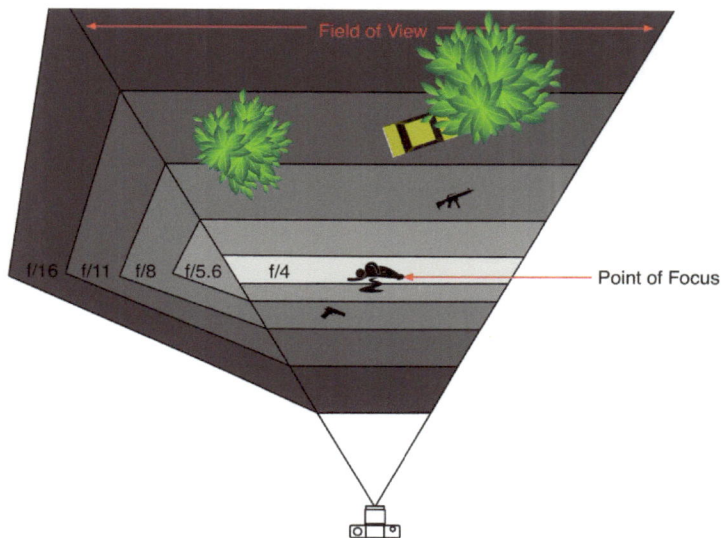

Note that approximately 1/3 of the Depth of Field is in front of the point of focus.

Hyperfocal Distance

The Hyperfocal Distance designates the point of focus that gives you the closest possible focus distance and also maintains focus all the way to infinity. There is a single Hyperfocal Distance for each combination of aperture and focal length. For example, the Hyperfocal Distance for f/8 at 35mm is 25' 2" and has a close focus point of 12' 8". This means that if you focus at 25' 2", everything from 12' 8" to infinity will be in focus. As long as you compose your shot so there is nothing closer than 12' 8" in the frame, everything in the frame will be in acceptable focus.

Calculating Depth of Field and Hyperfocal Distance

The Excel spreadsheet fcalc.xlsx, located at the link listed at the beginning of the book, will calculate Depth of Field and Hyperfocal Distance for you.

To calculate it manually, you need to know the constant for *Circles of Confusion*. For any DX or FX format camera, the constant value of .02 is sufficiently precise for anything we will be doing[10]. The math is as follows:

First, convert your focus distance from Feet to Millimeters:
Distance = FocusDistance * 308.4

Hyperfocal = (FocalLength * FocalLength) / (Aperture * Circles_of_Confusion)
NearPoint = (HyperFocal * Distance) / (HyperFocal + (Distance - FocalLength))
FarPoint = (HyperFocal * Distance) / (HyperFocal - (Distance - FocalLength))
TotalDoF = FarPoint – NearPoint

Finally, multiply your result by 0.00328084 to convert back to feet.

When using the spreadsheet, all you have to enter is the f/stop, the focal length, and the distance to the focal point in your frame.

---

[10] If you want to be exact, a DX camera is 0.019948 and an FX camera is 0.02501

Flash Modes

Flash can be used as your primary light source or as a supplemental light source. Many are what are called "dedicated" flash units. This means that they are designed for a specific set of cameras. By dedicating themselves to only these cameras, they can integrate more functionality than if they were trying to work with all cameras.[11]

One of the basic issues in flash photography is that for normal exposures shutter speed is now irrelevant. If you are using a flash, set your shutter to $1/60^{th}$ of a second and leave it there. You will adjust your exposures using the ISO, f/stop and flash output.

We use our flash units in one of three modes:
- Through the Lens (TTL)
- Through the Lens/Balanced fill (TTL/BL)
- Manual (M)

TTL and TTL/BL has effectively replaced an archaic "A/G" ("Automatic" or "Guide Number") mode that will not be used[12]. It is basically a 1st generation TTL locked in to a distance range. If you are outside of the set range, you are guaranteed an over or under exposed image. Since you need to check your setting each shot to be sure the range is correct, you might as well get better results and more precise control shooting Manual mode.

In TTL mode, the camera assumes that the flash is the primary light source and meters the flash output through the lens (hence the name), telling the flash to shut off after sufficient light has been received (yes, that's some very fast talking!).

In TTL/BL mode, the camera assumes the flash is the secondary light source and is being used to "balanced fill" the shadows. Again, it meters the flash output through the lens and tells the flash to shut off when light output is sufficient.

In Manual mode, the photographer sets the flash output power directly. He calculates what will make a proper exposure given the ISO, f/stop and distance of the subject or calculates the f/stop from the flash output, ISO and distance.

Why use M at all?
- TTL meters reflected light. Many times we can't tell what was most reflective in the frame until we look at the resulting image. If our subject was not the most reflective item in the frame, it will be underexposed.

---

[11] One of the primary dedicated features, which we will cover here, is Through The Lens (TTL) metering.
[12] Any situation in which A/G works, TTL or TTL/BL will work better. In any situation TTL or TTL/BL fails, A/G will fail just as badly or worse.

- When TTL fails, it fails miserably, often times leaving you with completely unusable images. Knowing what makes TTL fail allows you to compensate for it. Some of these situations are:
  - Large or bright reflective surfaces close to the camera.
  - Large mirrors at an angle to reflect the flash back to the camera.
  - Large windows letting in bright light.
  - Very bright lights.
  - Pinpoints of light in an otherwise dark frame.
  - When the camera is in Manual mode.

Flash output power is measured in stops (sound familiar?). You start at full power (designated M1/1) and divide by 2 until you reach the power level you need from the following:

M1/1, M1/2, M1/4, M1/8, M1/16, M1/32, M1/64, M1/128

All flash units go to M1/32 and some go as far as M1/128, giving us a total of 6 to 8 stops of output power adjustment. Many units will also adjust to third stops, designated as "+/-0.3EV" and "+/-0.7EV". For example, "M1/4 -0.7EV" is 2/3 stop less than ¼ power output.

Flash units are rated by Guide Numbers (GN)[13]. Some units have multiple guide numbers that depend on factors such as focal length and camera sensor size. To calculate flash output, you must know your guide number(s). Once you have this information, you calculate one of the following formulas:

f/stop = (Guide number x ISO Sensitivity Factor) / Shooting Distance
Shooting Distance = (Guide number x ISO Sensitivity Factor) / f/stop

ISO sensitivity factors:

ISO	25	50	100	200	400	800	1600	3200	6400
Factor	0.5	0.71	1	1.4	2	2.8	4	5.6	8

The spreadsheet flash distance.xlsx, located at the link provided at the beginning of the book, will do all these calculations for you once you have consulted your flash manual for the appropriate Guide Numbers.

---

[13] The guide number is the distance at which you would get a properly exposed image if you could set your camera to an f/stop of f/1.0. To properly interpret your GN value, you need to know if it is in feet or meters, and what ISO it is for.

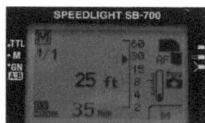

SPEEDLIGHT SB-700

25 ft

35 mm

This image is showing settings of M1/1, 35mm & a 25 foot flash to subject distance.

Technology bonus: On newer (SB-700 and higher) Nikon Speedlights, as well as some Canon units, the flash to subject distance is automatically calculated and displayed on the flash itself. (This only works if the flash is in the 90° straight forward position.)

Flash distance is a stickler – it is the distance from the flash to the subject, not the distance of the *camera* to the subject. Also, if you are using bounce flash the entire distance from the flash to the bounce surface to the subject needs to be accounted for when calculating.

Fill flash is used when a proper exposure, except for shadows, can be obtained without the flash. Fill flash can be done in TTL mode or Manual mode. Fill flash illuminates the shadowed areas to reveal detail without overpowering the overall exposure of the image.

Off-camera flash accomplishes several things. The flash can be manipulated so it does not reflect back into the image as a hot-spot when photographing glass or a mirror. It can be raised, lowered, or otherwise positioned to eliminate shadows in the image. It can be positioned past an object that is close to the camera that would otherwise cause a washed out hot-spot in the image. It can be positioned into an area to give it full illumination where an on-camera flash would be obstructed by the entrance. It can be pointed directly into the shadows in a fill flash scenario. It also enables the camera to see what you have found using oblique light. When using a flash off-camera, pay attention to the orientation of the flash in relation to the camera. If you have a horizontal camera and a vertical flash you may very well end up with heavy shadows in the periphery of your shot because of the way the light was focused.

Paint With Light

When flash is insufficient but artificial light is required, we "Paint with Light." There are several ways we can do this, and mastery requires practice.

In a large *indoor* environment, as long as you have at least one SB-700, SB-800, SB-900 or SB-910 flash unit to act as a master/controller, you can use Nikon's built in "Creative Lighting System" which uses infrared light to control an unlimited number of flash units (all of the previously mentioned models, plus the SB-600 which can only operate as a slave) from one controller. Using multiple flashes placed strategically throughout the scene then results in much more light than a single flash can produce distributed across a much larger area. Because it uses infrared light to trigger the remote flashes, this system only works indoors or in other scenarios such as a pavilion where the controlling light can be reflected back to the remote flashes. As with any advanced technique, practice is necessary.

To use remote flash units in an outdoor environment requires radio transceivers such as the PocketWizard FlexTT5. Unless all flash units are in TTL or a preset manual mode, a master/controller flash is still required.

The "classic" paint with light scenario involves manually firing a single flash unit multiple times from multiple locations in a single image. After calculating flash output, you can determine the locations that would give you overlapping flash patterns. With the shutter locked open in Bulb mode and an assistant holding a light block of some type covering the lens (such as a clipboard), you would go to each of your predetermined spots, have the assistant uncover the lens, manually fire the flash and have your assistant cover the lens again while you continue to the next spot. After firing the flash at all of the locations, release the lock and allow the shutter to close.

Another paint with light scenario involves locking the shutter open in Bulb mode and then using a light source such as a flashlight or the searchlight from a vehicle to "paint" the area with light. Because you do not have a calibrated output, the speed of your movement of the light through the scene and the length of the exposure are trial and error. Once the optimum speed of movement and overall exposure is found, a fully lit, properly exposed image will result.

Other Lighting Techniques

When the item you are photographing has harsh shadows on it, it is often easier to create shade than to try to over-power the shadows with flash. This can be as simple as having an assistant stand between the object and the light source, having an assistant hold a piece of cardboard to block the light, or as complex as setting up canopies.

When using oblique angles, your flash will project a shadow on the off side of the object. Using a reflector to bounce the light back onto the object from the other side will mitigate the shadow, resulting in a much better photograph. For small items, this can be as simple as an index card placed facing the flash, just outside the frame. Larger items may require some creative thought, such as a piece of poster-board or a white bed sheet stretched taut over a piece of cardboard or other frame.

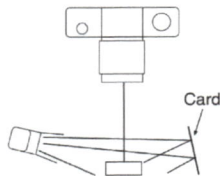

Card

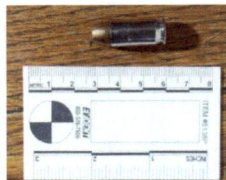

Off-side shadow mitigated
by bounce card reflector

Putting it all Together

Program Mode

Carry your camera in "P" (Program) mode at ISO 400. In this mode, the camera makes the exposure decisions, and if something happens fast, you can grab your camera, turn it on, and shoot without thinking – hopefully obtaining a useable image. Think of it as "P" = "Patrol Mode." If you need flash and you turn your flash on (or pop up the built-in flash), the camera will automatically calculate for it.

Auto Mode

"Auto" is not good because it will always assume you want flash. If you do not have an external flash connected and turned on, it will pop up the built-in flash. In most of our "grab and shoot" situations, we will be trying to cover much too much distance for flash to be useful. In fact, flash can cause us not to get what might otherwise have been a useable image.

Shutter Priority Mode

In Shutter priority Mode, you determine the desired shutter speed and the camera calculates the correct aperture setting. Because the aperture (f/stop) determines the Depth of Field this is control you do not want to give to the camera for the type of photography you do. There may be an application in surveillance work, but not in crime scene work. You should never have your cameras set to Shutter Priority Mode.

Aperture Priority Mode

In Aperture Priority Mode, you determine and set the aperture while the camera calculates the shutter speed. The camera will also calculate for flash if a dedicated unit is used. This is very convenient as you move about the scene concentrating on composition and depth of field issues, letting the camera take care of the shutter setting to make a proper exposure. The things to keep in mind with Aperture Priority Mode are:

1. Watch your shutter speed. When it drops below 1/60th second, it is time to deploy the tripod so your images do not blur due to camera shake. (You can increase your ISO, but insure you do so within the capabilities of your camera to produce a quality image.)

2. When you get to long exposures, watch carefully as you approach 30 seconds since this is the limit of most cameras. If it reads 30 seconds, consult the exposure meter. If the exposure meter is indicating under exposure, you will need to introduce additional light or switch to Manual mode, Bulb or Time, and calculate the correct exposure.
3. In a very complex scene (from a lighting perspective), even with Matrix metering Aperture mode can get confused, resulting in a poorly exposed image.

Manual Mode

In Manual Mode, you determine everything and the camera calculates nothing. The exception to this is if you are using TTL flash. In that case the camera will calculate the flash duration, though "interesting" results often occur. If you get wrapped up in what you are doing and forget to check exposure for every image, you can end up with a lot of useless images. When should you use Manual mode?

1. When the lighting is complex and you need to manually calculate the exposure after spot metering different parts of the frame.
2. For all Examination Quality photography. *This includes switching to manual focus!*
3. When you need to exceed a 30 second shutter speed. Going past 30 seconds will engage a shutter mode called "Bulb[14]" where you can release the shutter and hold it open for any arbitrary amount of time, or "Time" mode where one shutter press opens the shutter and a second one closes it, for up to 30 minutes. Timekeeping responsibility is transferred from the camera to the photographer in this mode. When you use Bulb mode, do not attempt to actually depress and hold the shutter button. Even with a heavy, stiff tripod this will introduce movement which will blur the image; instead you need to use a cable release – preferably one with a shutter lock, because the infrared remote shutter releases do not give you the ability to lock the shutter open. If all you have is an infrared release, use Time instead.

Using a flash limits your distances. Use the provided spreadsheet to calculate it. When used outside or in other large areas, bear in mind that anything past the calculated range is going to drop off in exposure rapidly. This is never desirable in a crime scene photo, so you should consider long exposure or paint with light if needed.

Once on a scene, you will want to use "A" (Aperture) or "M" (Manual) mode. Aperture mode is more convenient than Manual mode for exposures up to 30 seconds[15]. Always set your ISO manually depending on what your photographs will be. For general purpose work, ISO 400 should be your setting. This is the best balance between image quality and light sensitivity.

---

[14] Based on the original cable releases which used a rubber bulb to compress air that depressed the shutter. As long as you kept the bulb squeezed, the shutter stayed open.
[15] Depending on the shutter speed limitations of your camera.

Types of photography

The photographs taken by a Crime Scene Investigator differ in several ways from the photographs taken by other photographers. We are not concerned with artistic merit. We are not concerned with "flattering" lighting. We are concerned with accuracy. Accuracy in perspective. Accuracy in color. Accuracy in focus. Accuracy in content. Many times the "best" photographs we take are anything but artistic or flattering. Many times they are actually graphic and garish. Our photographs don't need to "strike a mood" – they need to depict the truth to the best of our ability.

Our photography breaks down into several types, each with it's own emphasis and challenges. These types, as defined by the systematic approach, are: Establishing, Overall, Midrange, Close-up, Supplemental and Examination Quality. We will go over each type, covering the intent as well as what some of the challenges are.

Establishing Photograph(s)

These photographs are used to establish the location of the scene. They can be anything that unequivocally identifies the location – a pair of street signs at an intersection (perhaps with the scene itself in the background), the address placard on the front of a building, the pole number from a GPS located utility pole, or any other readily identifiable fixed and permanent object. Depending on the location, size and complexity of a scene, there may be one Establishing Photograph, or an entire series leading from a known point to the scene proper. The photographs must be able to stand on their own, leading someone to the scene completely from their own content. Establishing Photograph(s) are taken during the initial phase of the systematic approach and are often the very first photographs taken on a scene.

Challenges include getting sufficient information in a single photograph to make it stand alone, or to insure enough overlap between the images that the location is not ambiguous. At night lighting becomes an issue as we are typically trying to cover an area much too large to use a flash. Long exposure and paint with light are both useful in these situations.

Establishing Photographs are taken at normal lens or wide angle from a natural perspective.

Overall Photographs

Overall Photographs, aka "overalls", are a series of photographs that depicts the entirety of the scene. Depending on the scene, there may be Outer, Inner, Outside, Inside and possibly more series of photographs. To be complete, the overalls must encompass the entire scene, inside and out as applicable, allowing an investigator or juror the ability to see the entire scene at some level of detail from just these photos. If you are unable to get enough distance from your scene to contain the entire view in one image, take overlapping images as necessary to capture the entire perspective. Overall Photographs are taken during the initial phase of the systematic approach. Overall Photographs can be taken before, after, or in conjunction with Establishing Photographs.

Overall Photographs present challenges in attempting to cover large areas, often at night, with the typical plethora of police activity in and around the scene. Use of a flash is often impractical if not impossible. Long exposure and paint with light are two useful techniques here.

Overall Photographs are taken at normal lens when they cover a distance of 30' or more. Wide angle is used when the distance is less than 30'. Overall Photographs should be taken from a natural perspective.

Midrange Photographs

Midrange photographs are taken of evidence during the collection phase, before the close-up photographs. Ideally they are taken from 7 – 10 feet away from the evidence with a fixed and permanent object in the frame, composed in such a manner that the relative position to the fixed and permanent object can be easily visualized with a reasonable degree of accuracy.

The primary complication with midrange photographs is the fixed and permanent object, which can often be some distance away, requiring long exposure photography or paint with light.

Midrange photographs should be taken at normal lens when possible and wide angle when necessary, from a natural perspective.

Close-up Photographs

There are two types of close-up photographs that must be taken of each and every piece of evidence. The first is in-situ, as found, undisturbed[16], without scale. When taking this photograph, it should be composed so that the next photo, the close-up with scale, can be taken with the exact same composition. When possible, this shot should be taken from a position perpendicular to and immediately above the item.

After the initial close-up you should take another close-up with scale. The scale should be arranged next to, but not touching, the item. The scale should be appropriately sized for the item and oriented with the long axis of the item being photographed. The scale and the item

---

[16] When our helpful citizen or patrol officer brings you an item, you can ask them to show you where they found it, but NEVER put it back in place to take the "in situ" photograph. The photograph itself is an integrity violation, and should it come out during a trial, can destroy the integrity of every piece of evidence you were involved in, for every case you have ever worked! If you didn't get the shot, you didn't get the shot – NEVER fake it! Even if it is something you inadvertently moved yourself, document the error, and move on.

must be on the same focal plane[17]. It should be obvious in the resulting image that the scale is not touching the item of evidence, so watch your perspective. When possible, this shot should also be taken from a position perpendicular to and immediately above the item. When this is not possible, the photo is taken in situ and then supplemental photography is done.

Close-up photographs should be taken at normal lens.

Supplemental Photographs

Supplemental photographs can be taken any time, but should be considered for the following circumstances at a minimum:
1. When a perpendicular close-up/close-up with scale could not be taken in situ, a close-up with scale should be taken from a perpendicular perspective immediately after collection and before packaging.
2. When additional detail can be documented from other angles, such as both sides of a knife blade.
3. To document the head-stamps of cartridges or cartridge cases.
4. To document any detail not seen in situ.

Supplemental photographs can be taken at the scene, or in your workspace before final packaging. A neutral background[18] should be employed for all supplemental photography. If, while packaging, additional detail is noticed, packaging should stop and supplemental photography of that detail should be conducted. Once the initial close-up without scale has been taken, all further photography of any evidence item should include a scale.

Supplemental photographs can be taken at normal lens, at full zoom, with close-up rings, or with a macro lens as appropriate.

Examination Quality photography

Any time that you are taking photographs that will be used by a forensic scientist for comparison, identification, or exclusion, the game changes. This is what is called "Examination Quality" and issues such as size, perspective, distortion, and the ability to do 1:1 reproduction for examination and comparison become critical. ISO 400 and hand-held are no longer sufficient. This generally pertains to 2D or 3D impression evidence, but it also applies to any evidence items you cannot collect or is so fragile you need to document it before any attempt to collect and transport it is made. Here are the rules for examination quality photography:

1. ISO 100.
2. Insure the camera is set for maximum image size and quality.

---

[17] This why you carry Play-doh in your kit – to make a platform for the scale(s) when photographing 3 dimensional objects.
[18] Butcher paper, paper bag, manilla folder, etc.

3. Shoot in RAW mode. RAW + JPEG mode if you have it.
4. Normal lens. (35 or 50mm) Use a prime (fixed) lens if available.
   a. When using a zoom lens, check the focal length between each shot so you catch and avoid any lens creep that may occur.
   b. If you know you have a lens creep issue, you can tape the focus and zoom rings into place after you are completely set up and focused.
5. Use a tripod.
6. Turn off Vibration Reduction.
7. Use a cable release for the shutter.
8. The axis of the camera lens must be exactly perpendicular to the subject.
9. Do initial setup away from horizontal impressions. Use your scale(s) to estimate framing.
10. For horizontal or vertical items or impressions, use a level to keep your setup as precise as possible.
11. Use flash.
12. Use a remote flash cable.
13. Insure you do not deflect the tripod when stretching the flash cable.
14. Create shade if necessary.
15. First shot is as found, without scale.
16. 4 directions
    a. As close to 90° apart as your setup allows.
17. 3 angles
    a. For 3D use moderate angles (85, 60, 45).
    b. For 2D use shallow angles (90, 80, 70).
    c. Experiment with angles as needed to see what gets the most detail.
18. Minimum of 13 exposures per impression/item.
19. Full manual camera control, to include focus and flash.
    a. f/11 or higher if possible[19].
    b. 1/60th second shutter.
    c. Calculate flash output.
       i. Remember that you are skimming the light across your subject and not getting the full output. Test and compensate as necessary. A good starting point is to calculate for half again more distance than you actually have.
    d. Be cognizant of your tripod legs and adjust flash direction as necessary to avoid shadows.
20. Insure the flash burst illuminates the entire item or impression.
21. Scale(s) must be on the same plane as the item or impression.
22. To the maximum extent possible, fill your frame.
23. Utilizing the RAW file, convert the image to a TIFF file for laboratory submission according to their guidelines.

Hot-shoe level

---

[19] Remember that your depth of field will decrease exponentially as your camera-to-subject distance decreases. For a deep impression, calculate DoF to be sure you will get what you need.

Portraits

A discussion of portrait photography may seem odd in a book on crime scene photography, however, there are times we may need to take photographs of victims or suspects for identification purposes. A photograph of a person's face taken at normal lens, or even full zoom on a typical kit lens, will have significant distortion of the nose, cheekbones and ears, resulting in an image that is often quite unlike the person's actual appearance. You will obtain the most natural appearance of a face by using an 85mm lens on a DX camera or a 120 to 135mm lens on an FX format camera. If you need to deviate from these focal lengths, longer lengths will be a better choice than shorter lengths.

Complex Lighting

Dynamic Range

This is where we have to touch on a little bit of theory. As used in this context, Dynamic Range means the difference (in f/stops) in lighting that a device can discern between what it renders as fully black and fully white.

The human eye is an amazing device. When fully adjusted and fixed on a single scene, it can discern a dynamic range of 12 to 14 f/stops – but when is the last time your eye was fixed on one spot? The eye is constantly adjusting and adapting. This gives a perceived dynamic range of up to 24 f/stops.

Cameras do not perform anywhere near as well as the human eye. The typical DSLR camera will have a dynamic range of 4 to 6 f/stops[20]. Use 4 f/stops as a good working figure. What this means is that if your darkest shadows and brightest highlights spot-meter within 4 f/stops of each other, you can select a middle value and get detail throughout your entire image. If they are more than 4 f/stops apart, you need to decide which part of the image is more important and select your exposure accordingly. If the entire image is equally important, you may need to take more than one image, exposing one to get details from the shadows and the other to get details in the highlights. In an extreme case, a third exposure to capture the mid-tone detail may also be called for.

High Dynamic Range Photography

High Dynamic Range (HDR) photography is an editing technique where multiple images with differing exposures are combined into a single image that covers the full dynamic range of all of the images. Using this technique[21], images with a dynamic range of 10 or more f/stops can be created. When taking images with the intention of creating an HDR image, shoot RAW, use a tripod to insure the composition of each image is identical, switch to manual focus so it does not change between the images, and keep the same f/stop setting for all of the images. Adjust the exposure only with the shutter speed. Do not use flash.

While there is no current case law pertaining specifically to HDR photography, there is ample case law concerning digital enhancement, and ultimately, you will be able to authenticate the photograph as a "fair and accurate representation of the scene." As in any editing scenario, maintain the original images in an unmodified form and document which images and what process you used to create the resulting HDR image.

---

[20] Some high end, multi-thousand dollar professional grade cameras have been reported as having a dynamic range as high as 10 f/stops.

[21] As with editing in general, there are many tools available and they all operate differently.

Alternate Light Source

Evidence found with an ALS can be photographed with the same ALS. First, take a photograph of the area or item normally. If you have a screw-on filter the same color as the goggles you are using, place it on your lens. If you do not have the appropriate screw-on filter, you can hold the goggles in front of your lens[22]. Illuminate the item with the ALS, meter through the filter or goggles, and take the photograph. If necessary, use a tripod. You can also use the ALS as you would a flashlight in a paint with light scenario.

Highly Reflective Surfaces

Off camera flash is invaluable in this situation, however, you often still get a reflected hot-spot that interferes with the image. Options include reflecting and diffusing the light. To reflect the light, fire the flash across the object towards a piece of poster-board or other reflective surface which is angled towards the subject. To diffuse the light, fire the flash through a piece of paper or white cloth. You can also build a "wall" of paper around the object and fire the flash into the paper from the side. Another option for diffusion is to cut the bottom off of a white plastic milk jug to place it over the object and cut off enough of the top for the lens to fit into. Fire the flash from the side and the plastic will diffuse the light all the way around the object.

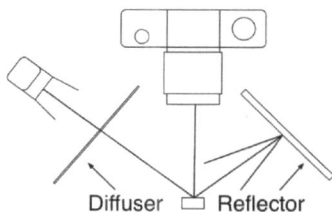

Diffusing and reflecting flash for a highly reflective object.

Lighting a Void

To direct light into a void, such as when photographing a piece of evidence in the bottom of a tin can, use a piece of glass above the void at a 45° angle. Aim the camera through the glass and fire the flash from a 90° angle. The glass will reflect some of the light down into the void and the camera will shoot the image through the glass. This technique is also effective for photographing prints or other 2D impressions on a mirror.

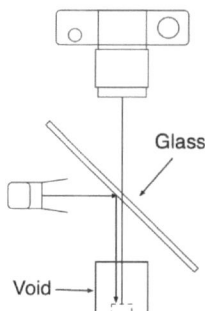

Using glass to reflect light into a void

---

[22] Clumsy, yes, but it works.

Reverse Lighting

When trying to photograph an item such as a fingerprint on a light bulb, placing the flash opposite the item from the camera and using a piece of paper to diffuse the light will back-light the bulb and make the developed print visible without any glare or reflection issues.

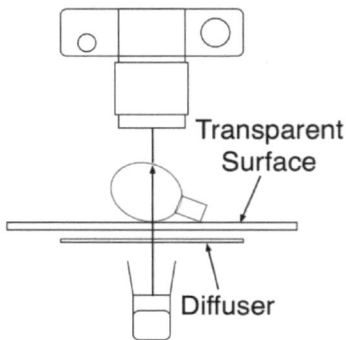

Reverse lighting

Luminol / BlueStar

Luminol and BlueStar are chemical solutions that have a luminescent reaction with blood. You can use them not only to find invisible traces of blood, but also to photograph them.

First, set up on a tripod and take a normal photograph of the area you want to treat. Shoot full manual and calculate manual bounce flash for this photograph. ISO 400 and f/8 are the preferred settings here.

Once you have taken the initial photograph, turn off your auto-focus, set your white balance to flash, and reduce your flash power one full stop. Set your shutter speed to Bulb. Make the environment as dark as possible – pitch black works best. (Quite unlike on TV, the luminescence of these chemicals is *very* faint.) Have an assistant spray the area being photographed and open your shutter. Be ready, because your flash will fire. Keep your shutter locked open for one to five minutes depending on the intensity of the reaction (one to three minutes for BlueStar or three to five minutes for Luminol is typical). Have your assistant re-spray the area every 20 to 30 seconds. Once you close your shutter, evaluate your image and adjust if necessary.

Some issues you will encounter:

You need to strike a balance when spraying the chemicals. Too little and you will get insufficient luminescence. Too much and the blood traces will run, or be absorbed to the point they are invisible. The area being sprayed needs to be covered uniformly so your reaction is consistent.

If you can see the person standing next to you, it might not be dark enough to get a good result. If you find the area during the day and you don't have the good fortune of a windowless room, you may very well have to wait until night time to get the shot. You can try covering all windows with black trash bags and cardboard to see if you can make it dark enough.

Some photo-luminescent tape on the legs and center column of your tripod may prevent an accident if people are trying to move around you in the dark.

If you are not in a place conducive to bounce flash, make a large diffuser for your flash out of paper.

Control the area. One knucklehead with a flashlight will ruin the shot for you in an instant.

Practice. Because we do not have a calibrated way to measure the intensity of the reaction, exposure times are going to be based on your judgement. The only way to get this experience is to see and do.

White Balance

I am addressing white balance here because it is typically in complex lighting scenarios that it becomes an issue.

Very simply, white balance is your camera adjusting to the light in your photograph so that white actually appears white in the final image. Most of the time, the automatic white balance setting will work quite well. *Most* of the time. You will recognize that you need some help in the white balance area when your images get a blue, green or yellow-orange color cast to them. When this happens, switch the camera to the appropriate preset white balance setting. These typically include: sunny, cloudy, overcast, tungsten lighting (incandescent light bulbs), fluorescent lighting, candle light, and flash. There is also usually a custom setting which you can set to the exact environment using a piece of white paper or an 18% grey card.

The simplicity of it is this – try different settings until white looks white in your photographs. Incidentally, snow, even in bright sun, often comes out best using the overcast setting.

Another reason to always shoot RAW is that you can *change* the white balance on a RAW file *after* you have taken the shot. Coming back to the workspace to discover all of your images are blue (or green or orange) is an easy fix, *if you shot them in RAW*. If you shot them in JPEG, they can still be adjusted, but at the expense of a lot of time and work.

Using Histograms

Histograms display the distribution of the brightness of pixels across the dynamic range of your camera in your image. As you can see from the example above, the left side indicates pure black and the right side indicates pure white. The higher the bar, the more pixels there are in that range. While the histogram can't tell you a "correct" exposure, it will show you the distribution of light in the image. While not an end-all, or even a go/no-go, the histogram is used for determining things like shadows being too dark or highlights being too bright. They are a useful tool on your belt and the more you use them, the more helpful they will be.

This histogram shows a good dynamic range, a fairly bright image, with no black shadows (hard left) and no blown highlights (hard right). You can tell this is a bright image by the large spike in the right quarter of the histogram.

The histogram to the right shows an overall well exposed photograph, but note the significant spike caused by the bright white scale card, almost to the point of blown highlights. Without the spike, this would be nearly a "perfect" histogram.

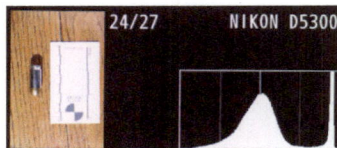

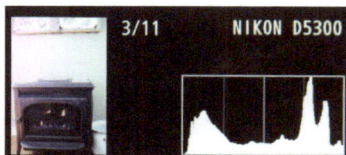

This histogram shows an image that just exceeds the dynamic range of the camera. It indicates a significant dark area but no totally black shadows, a bright area, and a few blown highlights where the graph hits the right limit. If those highlights contained detail I needed, I would decrease the exposure to bring the top end back into range and add some fill flash to keep the shadows from going completely dark.

This final example shows a very dark image, however, it is one that has visible detail throughout. While it is likely useable as-is, this image could be lightened easily.

Histograms, much like the images they represent, often show extremes. "Ideal" histograms have smooth curves, uniform peaks, and fall completely within the dynamic range of the camera. "Ideal" histograms are also a rare sight outside of a studio[23]. Once you gain some experience using histograms, you will be able to evaluate if you got the exposure you're looking for with a quick glance.

---

[23] Even in the studio, a "perfect" histogram is never the goal, and histogram results should never be a driving force in your photography decisions.

Rules of Thumb

Sunny 16

In situations where you have a broken exposure meter, this rule can be used as a baseline to get a reasonably exposed daylight image.

1. Set your shutter speed to the reciprocal of your ISO, or the closest value to it.
    a. For example, ISO 100 would get a 1/125 shutter speed while ISO 400 would get a 1/500 shutter speed.
2. Set your aperture according to the following:
    a. Bright day, distinct shadows – f/16
    b. Bright, hazy, soft shadows – f/11
    c. Bright, cloudy, no shadows – f/8
    d. Overcast – f/5.6
    e. Heavy overcast – f/4
    f. Deep shade or heavy shadow – f/2.8
3. Bracket!

Bright and dark subjects

When the majority of your frame is filled with light or dark subjects, your exposure meter gets confused. (Remember, it expects 18% grey.) Reduce exposure for dark subjects. Increase exposure for light subjects. When in doubt, bracket!

Shutter speeds and motion

When dealing with shutter speeds, there are 2 kinds of motion to deal with: camera movement and subject motion. Two different rules apply:

To eliminate *camera* movement when shooting hand-held, the shutter speed needs to be the *faster* of 1/60th second, or the speed correlating to the reciprocal of the lens focal length. For example:

- Using an 18mm lens, the reciprocal is 1/18th second. 1/60th second is faster, so it is selected.
- Using a 35mm lens, the reciprocal is 1/35th second. Again, 1/60th second is our choice.
- Using an 85mm lens, the reciprocal is 1/85th second. This is faster than 1/60th second, so we will set our camera to the closest (or faster) shutter speed. In this case the closest whole stop is 1/125th second, or we could use the closest third stop, which is 1/100th second. 1/80th second is closer, but slower, so we go the other direction.
- For a 105mm lens, we would select 1/125th second as our minimum shutter speed.

To freeze *subject* motion, use the guidelines in the following table:

Subject	Shutter Speed
Walking person	1/125
Jogging person	1/250
Bicycle or vehicle up to 30 mph	1/500
Vehicle up to 60 mph	1/1000
Propeller powered aircraft	1/2000

Care and Feeding of Batteries

Batteries, both alkaline & rechargeable, dislike extremes in temperature. Excess heat can can cause the charge to deplete and even physically damage the battery. Extreme cold affects the batteries ability to deliver it's charge. Cold batteries can be warmed (***but never by direct heat!***), but there's not much you can do for an overheated battery other than put it in a cool place and wait.

The rule of thumb: if you are comfortable, your batteries are comfortable.

Consider bringing your equipment inside instead of leaving it in your vehicle when you are off duty. Also consider storing it in the cabin instead of the trunk of your vehicle when you are on duty. If your batteries overheat, set them aside and use other batteries. Test them after they have cooled. To warm cold batteries, put them inside your clothes and allow body heat to gently warm them. Up to nearly full body temperature, the warmer they are, the more of their output will be available. Above body temperature, you may exact some additional power output from the battery, but it will be at the expense of shortening the battery's life span.

There is absolutely no proof to the wives tale that keeping batteries in the refrigerator extends their life, however, keeping them under 100° F (38° C) prevents their life from being unnecessarily shortened. While freezing a battery can damage it, this requires a temperature of -58° F (-50° C), so it is not an issue most of us will need to deal with.

Modern rechargeable batteries are not affected by "memory" like the original NiCad batteries were. There is no reason not to bring your battery back up to full charge after every use. If your battery is hot or cold, allow it to reach room temperature before placing it in the charger.

Rechargeable batteries begin to lose their charge as soon as you take them out of the charger. How fast they lose their charge depends on the quality and age of the battery. If your equipment sits idle for extended periods of time, it is a good practice to top off the charge in your batteries monthly.

Odds & ends

- In the event you do not think you can get a properly exposed image, it is better to under expose and end up with a dark image that has hidden detail than it is to over expose your image and blow out detail with the highlights. (If any old-timers tell you it is better to over expose, they learned that rule back in the days of using film, and it is the opposite for digital!)
- When practicing, get in the habit of using a photo log for two reasons:
  - Because you write down every exposure, it makes you think about what you are doing, which should also have you evaluating *why*.
  - When you are reviewing your images off camera, it is a ready reference to see what you did for each one, quickly showing you what worked and what didn't.
- To the extent possible, insure that your photographs do not include any extraneous items. A partial list includes:
  - Your feet.
  - Your reflection.
  - Your equipment.
  - Other police personnel.
  - Victims or witnesses (unless they are the subject of the image).
  - Police vehicles.

Camera Setup

This is a list of my preferred camera settings as they apply to crime scene work.

Image Quality

I always shoot RAW + JPEG. The JPEG is quick and convenient for review or providing copies to associates. JPEG files can typically be viewed on any computer, tablet or smartphone. The RAW file is the one that gives you the full potential of your camera. If you need the RAW and only have the JPEG, you are out of luck.

Image Size

Like RAW + JPEG, you can always resize and shrink an image, but you can't create detail or resolution that simply isn't there. Always set your camera to shoot the largest image it is capable of taking.

Focus Mode

This is a matter of preference. I find that for me, single-servo mode works best in a static environment. Manual focus is easier to select with the switch on the lens or camera body instead of navigating menus to turn it on or off if that is available on your camera.

Auto-focus Area

As discussed in the text, only the single-point auto-focus gives us the control we need.

Auto-focus Illuminator

This can be a very handy feature, especially at night or in dark spaces. If you work predominately during the day, you can leave it off to prevent the battery drain and only turn it on as needed. Working almost exclusively at night, I leave mine turned on all the time. Not all cameras have this feature. Typical useful range is 5 to 10 feet. For longer distances you will need a flashlight or other light source for autofocus to work well.

File Number Sequencing

This setting is critical. If it is turned off, your file names reset to 0001 every time you change or format your memory cards. For example, Nikon file names are in the form of DSC_xxxx.JPG and DSC_xxxx.NEF. This creates a *huge* potential of accidentally overwriting images with different images bearing the same filename. With it turned on, you won't see 0001 again until you shoot your ten thousandth image after reaching 9999. You can work with and around it, but it adds significant complexity to your file management issues, and the responsibility to be aware of and manage it rest directly on your shoulders.

Long Exposure Noise Reduction

Try both with and without to determine the capabilities of your camera. With this turned on it takes significantly longer to write the images, but it may give a better quality image.

High ISO Noise Reduction

Exactly the same issue as long exposure noise reduction. Experiment with your equipment to see if the results are worth the additional time.

Frequently Asked Questions

1. My camera's exposure meter tells me the exposure is correct. What is it measuring?
   a. Your camera's exposure meter expects 18% reflectivity from a scene.
2. My scene is not an "18%" scene[24]. What can I do?
   a. Meter on an 18% Grey Card.
   b. Meter on the palm of a hand, then increase 1 stop.
   c. Meter on a field of grass.
   d. Meter on a clear blue sky, away from the sun.
   e. Use the "Sunny 16" rule of thumb; see page 30.
   f. Bracket
3. I am over/under exposed. What can I adjust?
   a. Any of f/stop, shutter speed, ISO or available/augmented light.
      i. If this is a regular issue, consider adjusting the exposure compensation on your camera. If it only happens when using flash, there is a flash-only exposure compensation setting.
4. If f/8 to f/11 is 1 stop, why does my camera show me f/9 and f/10 as well?
   a. These are 1/3 stop settings. You may also have 1/3 stop shutter speeds and ISO settings.
5. What are the stop values?
   a. See the stop table to the right.
6. I have to take a shot at slower than a 1/60th second shutter, but I don't have time to set up the tripod. What should I do?
   a. Take a second to evaluate – is there really no time, or is someone being impatient? If someone is being impatient, it's your scene – make them wait; do it right.
   b. Once you are sure you can't wait, use every precision marksmanship technique you have ever learned – especially follow-through. Brace your body into the most stable position possible, get good solid bone support on the camera, or rest it on a solid, immovable object[25]. Squeeze the shutter and FREEZE when it

Stop Table
(whole stops in bold)

Shutter Speeds	f/Stops	ISO Sensitivity
1/8000	**1.0**	**12**
1/6400	1.1	16
1/5000	1.2	20
1/4000	**1.4**	**25**
1/3200	1.6	32
1/2500	1.8	40
1/2000	**2.0**	**50**
1/1600	2.2	64
1/1250	2.4	80
1/1000	**2.8**	**100**
1/800	3.2	125
1/640	3.5	160
1/500	**4.0**	**200**
1/400	4.5	250
1/320	5.0	320
1/250	**5.6**	**400**
1/200	6.3	500
1/160	7.1	640
1/125	**8**	**800**
1/100	9	1000
1/80	10	1250
1/60	**11**	**1600**
1/50	13	2000
1/40	14	2500
1/30	**16**	**3200**
1/25	18	4000
1/20	20	5000
1/15	**22**	**6400**
1/13	25	8000
1/10	29	10000
1/8	**32**	**12500**
1/6	36	
1/5	42	
1/4	**45**	
1/3	50	
1/2.5	57	
1/2	**64**	
1/.6		
1/.3		
1		
1.3		
1.6		
2		
2.5		
3		
4		
5		
6		
8		
10		
13		
16		

---

[24] Examples would be snow, blacktop, large reflective surfaces, etc.

[25] A running vehicle is not a solid, immoveable object. The vibrations from the running engine are enough to cause camera shake and blur. If you must use a vehicle, be sure it is not running.

        releases. Do not even breath while the shutter is open. ANY movement at all will result in blurriness in the image.

7. My Nikon flash says TTL or TTL/BL and I don't seem to be able to change it. Why?
   a. The flash automatically selects between these two modes based on the *metering mode* you have set on the camera.
      i. In Matrix or Center Weighted metering, the flash sets for TTL/BL.
      ii. In Spot metering, the flash sets for TTL.
8. In TTL (or TTL/BL) mode, when I take a shot, the red light on the flash and the flash indicator in the viewfinder both blink. What doses this mean?
   a. This means that the flash has fired at full power, yet the meter has not indicated sufficient light was seen. You likely have an underexposed image. View the image, check the histogram, and adjust as necessary.
      i. Wider aperture.
      ii. Increased ISO setting.
      iii. Move flash closer to subject.
   b. You will not see this indicator when using the flash in manual mode.

Glossary

ABFO	American Board of Forensic Odontology
ABFO #2 Scale	An "L" shaped scale with a 90° angle, 80mm on each inside edge.
APS format	A camera with a sensor the same size as an APS film negative (25.1 x 16.7mm).
Bureau Scale	A Bureau scale is another "L" shaped scale with a 90° angle. It is 155mm on the short leg and 300mm on the long leg. It is called a Bureau scale because it was designed by the FBI. It has been largely adopted as the scale to use when photographing footwear impressions.
DX format	APS format sensor size.
Dynamic Range	The amount of variation, measured in f/stops, between full black and full white for a given device.
Fixed lens	Another name for a prime lens.
Flash Sync Speed	See Sync Speed.
Full frame	A camera with a sensor the same size as a 35mm film negative (24 x 36mm).
FX format	Full frame sensor size.
HDR Photography	A technique of combining differently exposed images that gives a higher dynamic range than is possible in a single image from any given device.
ISO	International Standards Organization.
ISO sensitivity	The sensitivity of the sensor to light, as defined by the ISO. The values for a digital sensor are equivalent to the values for film.

JPEG	Joint Photographic Experts Group. The image file format defined by JPEG, typically ending in an extension of .JPG. This image file has camera settings applied and has undergone a compression algorithm to reduce its size. The algorithm used is "lossy," so every time a JPEG image is saved, more detail is lost. It is used universally as a format for files where total preservation of all available detail is not a requirement.
Multiplier effect	The effect of a smaller sensor causing a lens to have the field of view of a higher focal length. On DX format Nikon cameras this is 1.5, so a 100mm lens would have the same field of view as a 150mm lens on a full frame camera. Most DX format Canon cameras have a 1.6 multiplier. Full frame or FX format cameras do not have this effect, but they also cannot use lenses designed specifically for DX format cameras. The multiplier effect is why a normal lens is 50mm for a FX format camera and 35mm for a DX format camera.
Natural Perspective	The perspective of the scene from a natural point of view. Photographs taken in a natural perspective are taken from the standing position with the camera brought up to eye level.
Normal lens	The focal length for the camera in use that gives the closest view to what the eye actually sees. This also correlates to the lens that will have a 45° field of view. For FX format cameras, it is 50mm. For DX format cameras, it is 35mm.
Prime lens	A lens with a single focal length. As opposed to a zoom lens.
RAW	The file format containing the data as it was generated by the sensor, without any processing. This is the format that represents the total capability of your camera. Settings such as white balance are not applied to the RAW file data. Nikon RAW files have a .NEF extension while Canon RAW files have a .CR2 extension. RAW files are either not compressed, or compressed with a lossless compression algorithm.
Sync Speed	Also Flash Sync Speed. The fastest speed a camera can operate its shutter and remain synchronized with a flash unit. At a faster speed, the flash will actually capture the shutter in the image. Typically, using a dedicated flash unit will yield a faster sync speed. The universally safe shutter speed for flash use is $1/60^{th}$ of a second.
TIFF	Tagged Image File Format. TIFF files typically end with the extension .TIF and is a popular format for large, highly detailed images. TIFF is

	used as a universally accepted format where RAW files are proprietary to each manufacturer. TIFF images are uncompressed.
Zoom lens	A lens that can be set to a value in a range of focal lengths. For example, an 18-55mm lens can be set at 18mm, 55mm, or any value in between.

Appendix

Sample Photo Log

Photo Log Page #___of____   **ISO**: 100-400
Light: (A) Available (M) Manual Flash (TTL)Auto (FL)Flashlight   **Focal Length**: 18mm, 35mm, 55mm, rings 1-7
Focus: Manual (M), or Auto (A)   **Special Tech**: (B) Bounce, (O) Oblique, (F) Fill, (D) Diffuse

Indicate retakes on log

#	DESCRIPTION	ISO	LIGHT	FOCUS	FOCAL LENGTH	SS	F-STOP	SPECIAL TECHS